Ellie's
Big Girl
Knickers

Rebecca
Ottaway

First published 2015

© Rebecca Ottaway 2015

becottaway@gmail.com

ISBN: 978-0-9944506-0-9

www.rebeccaottaway.com

Printed by Createspace

For my girls, Mouse and Boo who
keep me on my toes and for
my own Mother who looks down on me.
For my Husband always and forever.

E llie loved her mummy and she wanted to be just like her. They had the same hair, the same eyes and they even wore the same coloured dresses. But Mummy wore big girl knickers and Ellie wore nappies.

4

Ellie wanted to be a big girl too and she wanted to wear big girl knickers. But first, she needed to find some. She tried on Mummy's ... but they were too big. She found a pair of Grandma's ...

but they were far too big!

6

Ellie wondered, *would Daddy wear big girl knickers? No! He's not a girl.* She giggled to herself. Mummy suggested they go to the shops to buy Ellie her very own big girl knickers.

Mummy and Ellie went shopping at the department store. There were rows and rows of wonderful knickers. Some were plain, some had patterns, and some even had bows. Ellie's mummy bought seven pairs of knickers;

one for

each day

of the week.

Ellie loved all her new knickers, especially the ones for Sunday. They were soft to touch and easy to pull up and down. And they were not puffy and round like nappies.

B ut Ellie didn't want to wee in her new knickers.

'**Quick Mummy, nappy!**' Ellie called. Instead, Mummy took Ellie to the toilet.

14

The toilet seemed so big and high, and the hole so large! And what was that scary whooshing noise it made?

Mummy said not to worry, as she put a step close to the toilet and a special seat for Ellie.

"Wees and poos go in the toilet, not in your nappy or your knickers. When you get that feeling in your tummy that tells you your wees are coming, come straight to the toilet. Pull down your knickers and sit right up here."

Ellie wasn't sure about the toilet at all, but if her mummy could do it, then she could too.

18

Ellie was a little scared as she sat her bottom on the toilet. Unfortunately she missed and her wee went on the floor. The next time her wee came out before she had reached the toilet door. The third time well, ...

it was a disaster.

Mummy gave Ellie a hug and told her not to worry, she would soon make it.

The next day Ellie was playing at day care, when suddenly she had to go to the toilet. She looked down – new knickers! She looked up – no teachers!

Ellie had to go by herself.

22

So she ran from the sandpit ... hold it, hold it ... past the busy bee painting area ... hold it, hold it ... through the quiet-as-a-mouse storybook corner ... hold it, hold it ... and onto the toilet ...

Flush!

"Yes, I did it all by myself!" yelled Ellie. "I'm just like mummy, I'm a big girl now!"

About the Author

Rebecca Ottaway is a Gold Coast based author who also works as a Sales Marketing Executive. As a mother of two, she is extremely familiar with the challenges of toilet training. Being a passionate advocate for educational yet entertaining children's books, Rebecca felt it important to write engaging stories for girls and boys that addressed this aspect of growing up in a creative and realistic way. Rebecca hopes that her books will be helpful for parents and embraced by children.

18504487R00019

Printed in Poland
by Amazon Fulfillment
Poland Sp. z o.o., Wrocław